AND IT CAME TO PASS
TO PASS

Emmanuel

Narrations by Rose Aspinall. Transcriptions by Jay Rouse.
Orchestrated by Ed Hogan.
Editor: Chrislyn Reed • Music Engraving: David Thibodeaux • Cover Design: Jodi Hull

FOREWORD

Yes, it came to pass—the incarnation of the Word, the divine promise of God!

He came not in power but in weakness, not in wealth but in poverty.

And this was God's plan from the beginning. For it was out of His love and goodness that mercy was made visible to us by a Baby in a cradle.

Our need called out to His love and He came. Though we turned away from eternal things, He restored them to us in Jesus. We were eyewitnesses to His majesty!

And now, we eagerly await His return. Oh, wait but a little! Weeping may endure for a night, but joy comes in the morning.

For just as it came to pass in that day, the day has been set when He will come again.

For all that comes to us here on earth, comes to pass!

PRODUCT INFORMATION

30/3486MD	Full Score
30/3487MD	Set of Parts
30/3488MD	CD with Printable Parts
30/3489MD	Full Score and Parts plus CD with Printable Parts
65/2081MD	SATB Book
65/2082MD	SATB Score with Performance CD
99/3751MD	Stereo Accompaniment Track
99/3752MD	Split-track Accompaniment
99/3753MD	SA/TB Part-dominant Rehearsal CDs
99/3754MD	Bulk Performance CDs (10-pack)
99/3755MD	Stem Files Disc

1-800-444-1144 • www.lorenz.com

INSTRUMENTATION

All songs *(with the exception of Jesus, Prince of Peace and Joseph's Song)* include the following instrumentation:

Flute 1 & 2
Oboe *(Soprano Sax)*
Clarinet 1 & 2
Trumpet 1
Trumpet 2 & 3
Horn 1 & 2 *(Alto Sax)*

Trombone 1 & 2
  (Tenor Sax/Baritone T.C.)
Trombone 3 & Tuba
Harp
Violin 1 & 2
Viola *(Clarinet 3)*
Cello *(Bass Clarinet) (Bassoon)*

String Bass
Keyboard String Reduction
Drums
Percussion 1 & 2
Rhythm *(Piano/Guitar/Bass)*

Jesus, Prince of Peace – No Brass
Flute 1 & 2
Oboe *(Soprano Sax)*
Clarinet 1 & 2
Harp
Violin 1 & 2
Viola *(Clarinet 3)*
Cello *(Bass Clarinet) (Bassoon)*
String Bass
Keyboard String Reduction
Drums
Percussion 1 & 2
Rhythm *(Piano/Guitar/Bass)*

Joseph's Song – No Trumpets
Flute 1 & 2
Oboe *(Soprano Sax)*
Clarinet 1 & 2
Horn 1 & 2 *(Alto Sax)*
Trombone 1 & 2 *(Tenor Sax/Baritone T.C.)*
Trombone 3 & Tuba
Harp
Violin 1 & 2
Viola *(Clarinet 3)*
Cello *(Bass Clarinet) (Bassoon)*
String Bass
Keyboard String Reduction
Drums
Percussion 1 & 2
Rhythm *(Piano/Guitar/Bass)*

TABLE OF CONTENTS

ADESTE FIDELES

Words and Music by
JOHN FRANCIS WADE
Arr. by Jay Rouse

In the beginning was the Word.

The Word, enduring and eternal.

And the Word was with God.

The Word, righteous and holy!

And the Word was God—and all things were made by Him.

And God and man communed in ways deep and true—until the fall.

In one moment shame and guilt entered the created world. We separated ourselves from God. Mankind chose his course, while God chose His—the complete restoration of mankind.

And so it is that in the rising and falling of the years—years of light and of darkness, there has been and ever will be, but one constant.

The Word.

At the appointed hour, this Word, the very seal of His promise, breaks open and declares that He who has spoken is true.

Listen!

The Word became flesh—and dwelt among us. He is Jesus, the incarnate Word of God!

There is but One God. One Word. One Story.

And it came to pass!

14

65/2081&82MD-14

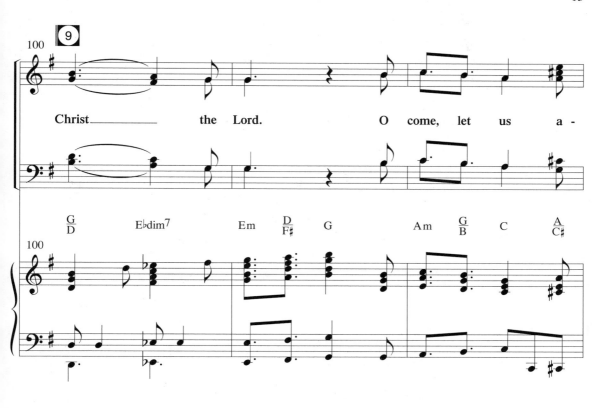

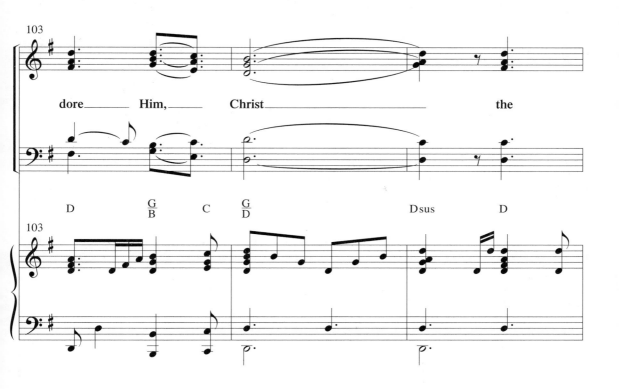

AND IT CAME TO PASS

Words by
ROSE ASPINALL

Music by
JAY ROUSE
Arr. by Jay Rouse

mong us now on earth. It came to pass! Em-man-u-

el!

Come

MEN unison **mf**

now,   you rich and   poor,   hear   the Ba - by's

cry.   The   Prince   of Peace, the   Lamb   of God   here

in   a sta - ble   lies.   Joy - ful_____

news_____ on earth to - day!_____ The

bright and morn - ing star has come to light the

way! And it came to pass that in

24

76
Word of God a - mong us now on earth. It came to
C2/E C/E Cm2/E♭ Cm/D♯ G/D Am/D G/D
79
17
pass! Em - man - u - el!
f Re -
Am/D G/D Am/D Gsus/D Gsus G
f
82
joice! Re - joice!
O come, Em - man - u - el. O come, Em -
joice! Re - joice!
O come, Em - man - u - el. O come, Em -
D Em D/F♯ Em/G D7/A Em/G D/F♯ B A7/C♯ B/D♯ D/F♯

26

man - u - el. Em - man - u -
man - u - el.

Em   B7 Em G/D Am/C   Am   Esus/B   B7

el!   And it came   to   pass   that in

E11   E   D/E   A E A

rit.   *ff*

those days   we saw   the Sav - ior   face to face. The

Bm/A   A   Esus   E   Bm/A   A

65/2081&82MD-26

JOSEPH'S SONG

**Words by
ROSE ASPINALL**

**Music by
JAY ROUSE**
Arr. by Jay Rouse

In Biblical history, one line alone is traced from the beginning, the line of King David. It was from this line that the Messiah would come.

There were fourteen generations in all from Abraham to David. There were fourteen from David until the exile in Babylon and after that fourteen generations more.

And within this line Jacob fathered Joseph. Joseph was the husband of Mary, and Mary was the mother of Jesus who is called the Messiah.

This is how the birth of Jesus came about: His mother Mary, was pledged to be married to Joseph, but before they came together, she was found to be with Child. Because Joseph, her husband, was faithful to the law, and yet did not want to expose her to public disgrace, he had in mind to divorce her quietly. But after he considered this, an angel of the Lord appeared to him in a dream.

"Joseph, son of David, don't be afraid to take Mary home as your wife. What is conceived in her is from the Holy Spirit. She will give birth to a Son, and you are to give Him the name Jesus, because He will save His people from their sins."

When Joseph woke up, he did what the angel of the Lord commanded him.

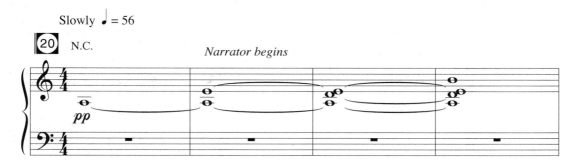

have a plan, though a mys - ter - y to me. I will

Ooo

Ebm7   Fsus   F/A   Bbm

set my feet up - on Your path, so You can set us

So You can set us

A2   Db/Ab   Ebm7

Jesus, What a Wonderful Child

TRADITIONAL
Arr. by Jay Rouse

See how at the appointed moment, God sets everything into place? The hour of His purpose strikes and unfulfilled prophecy is laid open. The fulfillment of His word comes to pass.

Just as God spoke in days of old, He speaks again! Dimly lit truth shines and dispels the darkness!

And now, the promise of new life! Hope ignites the ancient longing burning in the hearts of God's people!

Glory to the new born King!

"... the promise of new life!"

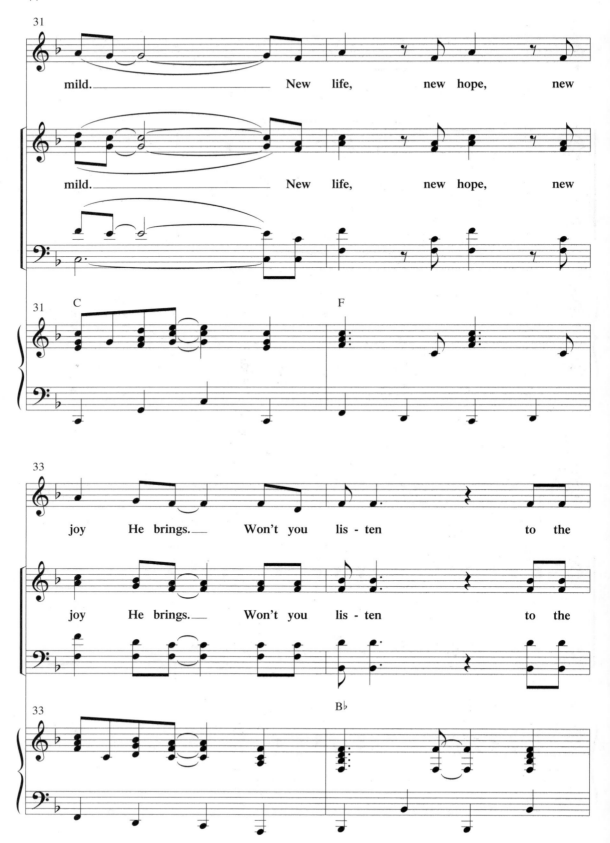

46

48

65/2081&82MD-48

CODA

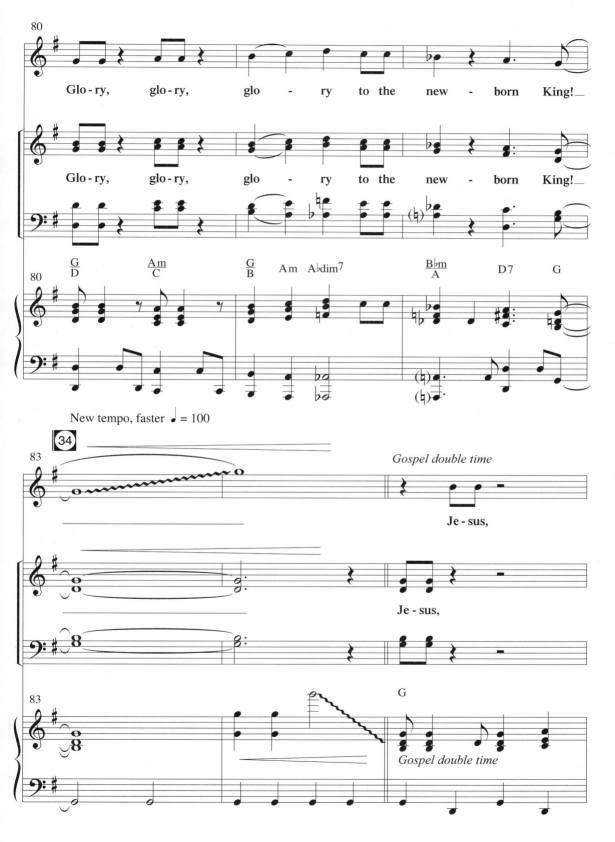

JESUS, PRINCE OF PEACE

with

AWAY IN A MANGER

Words by
ROSE ASPINALL

Music by
JAY ROUSE
Arr. by Jay Rouse

Listen to the words of the prophesy:

To us a Child is born! To us a Son is given! And the government will be on His shoulder.

He will be called the Wonderful Counselor! Mighty God!

Everlasting Father!

This Infant who brings eternity to earth will usher in His Kingdom of peace. This Child will lead us.

For contained within Him is all the love of the Father. Everything that we need to be reconciled to God can be found in Him.

Jesus, Prince of Peace!

12 ⟦38⟧ *"For contained..."*

"Jesus, Prince of Peace!"

CHOIR unison
warmly

Je - sus, Prince of Peace,_____ come here from

D²   Bm⁷

Heav - en our dark - ness to cease._____

G²

AWAY IN A MANGER *(McFarland/Murray)*

64

42

Je - sus, Prince of Peace,_____ come here from
our dark - ness to cease._____
Heav - en
In - fant Re - deem - er se - cures our re -

Fire in the Sky

Words by
ROSE ASPINALL

Music by
JAY ROUSE
Arr. by Jay Rouse

And it came to pass in those days, that there went out a decree from Caesar Augustus, that all the world should be taxed. And all went to be taxed, everyone to his own city.

Joseph also went up from Galilee, out of the city of Nazareth, into Judea, to the city of David, which is called Bethlehem because he was of the house and lineage of David. In nearby fields, the night fires of the shepherds had burned to embers when without warning the skies over Bethlehem flamed with unnatural light.

Leaping to their feet the shepherds shielded their faces! The sky was raining fire!

Then from out of the fire, a voice "Don't be afraid!"

"I bring you good news of great joy which shall come to all the people!"

And suddenly, they saw, not fire, but a host of angels filling the sky!

Glory to God in the highest! To you is born this day in the city of David, a Savior who is Christ the Lord!

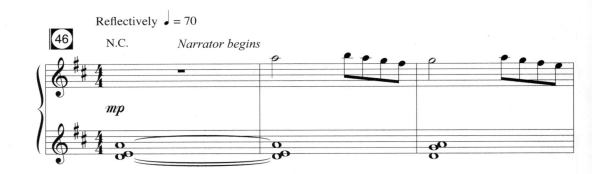

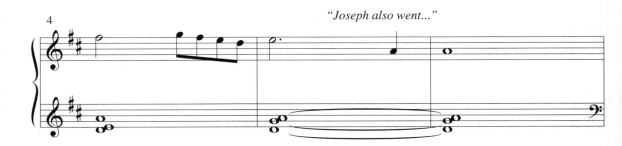

CHILD OF THE PROMISE

Words by
ROSE ASPINALL

**Music by
JAY ROUSE**
Arr. by Jay Rouse

It came to pass as the angels were gone away from them into Heaven, the shepherds said one to another, "Let us now go to Bethlehem and see this thing that has happened, which the Lord has made known to us."

And they went and found Him, come not in glory but in a stable.

He came not in power but in weakness, not in wealth but in poverty.

And this was God's plan from the beginning. For it was out of His love and goodness that mercy was made visible to us by a Baby in a cradle.

His perfect masterpiece of love.

"For it was out of..."

"... masterpiece of love."

Un - der the stars sleeps a Child of the prom - ise.

Com - mon made ho - ly, our God come to earth.

mp MEN unison

Glo - ry re - sid - ing here in a poor man - ger,

slight rit.

come to re - deem us and show us our— worth.

slight rit.

90

65/2081&82MD-90

f *O HOLY NIGHT (Dwight/Adam)*

96

98

65/2081&82MD-98

AND IT CAME TO PASS FINALE

Arr. by Jay Rouse

Yes, it came to pass—the incarnation of the Word, the divine promise of God. He was as the prophet foretold, a light shining in the darkness!

Our need called out to His love and He came! Though we turned away from eternal things, He restored them to us in Jesus. We were eyewitnesses to His majesty!

And now, we eagerly await His return. Oh, wait but a little! Weeping may endure for a night, but joy comes in the morning.

For just as it came to pass in that day, the day has been set when He will come again. For all that comes to us here on earth, comes to pass!

To Him be honor and glory and power forever! Amen!

104

65/2081&82MD-104

106

AND IT CAME TO PASS (Rose Aspinall/Jay Rouse)

© 2017 Lorenz Publishing Company, a division of The Lorenz Corporation.
All rights reserved. Printed in the U.S.A.

65/2081&82MD-106